But, in the eyes of these fi  ?
who were already there, the Nat /
of it. Only what the Europeans /
Spanish, French, Portuguese o ?
land.

Banksy completed the art work at the time when San Francisco City was passing a law forbidding anyone from sitting or lying on pavements. It was an attempt to stop street begging. Banksy's piece of art has now been whitewashed out to leave just the original 'No Trespassing' sign. The Native American peoples have been all but blotted out of their ancestral lands, almost but not quite.

At the museum which celebrates the Pilgrims' landing, *Plimouth Plantation,* there is a Wampanoag Homesite created by  and with the members of the Wampanoag Native American community to celebrate their culture and heritage. A leader of this community is Paula Peters (left), teacher and cultural ambassador for her people, the Mashpee Wampanoag. They were there when the Pilgrims landed. They still live in the area and have hung on to a small acreage of their 'tribal lands', in a small corner of Cape Cod. They are currently seeking Congressional approval for their territorial claim. Although their township of Mashpee was incorporated in 1870, their lands have not yet been recognised as a formal reservation, as the 'land in trust' of the Mashpee Wampanoag people.

The well-known quotation from the Native American Chief Seattle, from the far north-west of the USA, puts the conflict between the Native American view of the land and the European view like this:

'How can you buy or sell the sky, the warmth of the land? The idea is strange to us....The rivers are our brothers....The air is precious...for all things share the same breath and this we know. The earth does not belong to man. Man belongs to the earth. This we know. All things are connected like the blood which unites one family.'

So were the English who landed from the Mayflower and settled at Plymouth, trespassers? What about those who had come to found Jamestown in 1607, or all the other Europeans who had crossed the Atlantic to set up colonies on the North and South American coasts, were they trespassers? They did not think so. They believed that they had the right to occupy and exploit what they called 'the New World' because they thought of it as an empty land, ripe for occupation.

This must have been in William Bradford's thinking when he wrote about the Pilgrim Fathers' planning for their epic voyage:

'The Place they had thoughts on was some of those vast and unpeopled countries of America, which are fruitful and fit for habitation, being devoid of all civil inhabitants, where there are only savage and brutish men which range up and down, little otherwise than the wild beasts of the same.'
(from William Bradford's 'Of Plymouth Plantation' Ch4.)

And so we began our work on Mayflower 400 by asking a question about this Banksy, and by drawing our own versions of it:

Banksy painted the "NO TRESPASSING" piece of art because he saw a Native American under a 'no trespassing sign' in San Francisco in America. The next day he found a 'no trespassing' sign and painted what he had seen. He painted it again in London in 2012, meaning that the English trespassed on the Native American Indians' land, which they had lived on for generations. This incredibly tragic story inspired Banksy to create a piece of art to symbolise that even now, all of these years later, the Indians still have Americans trespassing on their land, and are ignored.

(by Studio 5/6, St Helena's CofE Primary School, Willoughby)

'My Banksy' by Mille E.

But who is Banksy?

Banksy is a famous graffiti artist, known only for his graffiti art but the rest of his identity, even his real name, is unknown. He does his work when no one is watching, like at night. At an auction, they were selling one of his drawings but Banksy was out of sight. As soon as it was sold, it got shredded; it raised the price even higher! But how did he do that? People even copy some of Banksy's artwork and successfully sell them for millions at auctions. But why does he want to be anonymous? He is known as 'invisible man' because he does his art at unknown places.

(by Studio 5/6, St Helena's CofE School, Willoughby)

8

2. Who are the Native Americans?

When the Virginia Company were granted a Charter by James I of England to establish a settlement on the shores of the New World, the Charter included these Instructions:

Instructions for the Virginia Colony

'When it shall please God to send you on the coast of Virginia, you shall do your best endeavour to find out a safe port in the entrance of some navigable river, making choice of such a one as runneth farthest into the land... and to the end that you be not surprised as the French were in Florida...and the Spaniard in the same place by the French, you shall do well to make this double provision. First, erect a little store at the mouth of the river that may lodge some ten men; with whom you shall leave a light boat, that when any fleet shall be in sight, they may come with speed to give you warning. Secondly, you must in no case suffer any of the native people of the country to inhabit between you and the sea coast; .... but they will grow discontented with your habitation, and be ready to guide and assist any nation that shall come to invade you; and if you neglect this, you neglect your safety.

In all your passages you must have great care not to offend the naturals,.........and imploy some few of your company to trade with them for corn and all other victuals if you have any; and this you must do before that they perceive you mean to plant among them; for not being sure how your own seed corn will prosper the first year, to avoid the danger of famine, use and endeavour to store yourselves of the country corn.

The English were most concerned that they should not be attacked and wiped out by either the Spanish or the French, both of whom already had settlements in North America. Those whom they called the 'native peoples' or 'naturals', they regarded as less of a threat and even as a help. Should their own attempts at growing food crops fail, these 'naturals' might even be a good source of the 'country corn' to avoid famine. There was no thought that these 'naturals' might in any way 'own' the land the English planned to occupy. Virginia had been claimed for the English in the name of the Virgin Queen, Elizabeth I, and no other 'Christian Prince' had a right to be there. The rights of the 'naturals' did not count.

But who were 'the naturals'? We now know that we all carry a great deal of information about our origins in our DNA and there are companies which will tell you about your racial heritage if you send them a sample of your DNA, and a fee!

Studies of the DNA of Native Americans have shown that they all carry a link to their origins in the extreme north-east of Siberia, the land to the east of the Bering Sea which now separates the continents of Asia and America.

When Europeans first met Native Americans,

they noticed that they looked different. Columbus called the inhabitants of the Caribbean island he first landed on 'Indians', because he thought he had reached the Indian sub-continent, but he was not totally wrong in attributing some Asian heritage to them. Some of the earliest images we still have of Native Americans show features which are clearly Asiatic.

These images above are of Algonquin women, Native Americans from what is now North Carolina. They were painted by John White, an English artist, in 1585 when he was a member of the English Colony which Raleigh tried to establish on their island. They are part of a collection of his work held in London in the British Museum. Both images show capable women with strongly Asiatic features. But how can we explain how Americans of Native American heritage still have in their DNA these links with people whose origin is in Siberia, the extreme north-east of the Asian continent?

According to a report which appeared in the London Times on June 7th 2019, genetic evidence of a close kinship between ancient Siberians and indigenous (Native) Americans has been confirmed after analysis of the fossils of two boys' 32,000-year old milk teeth. "This is the missing link between Old World populations and New World populations, between Native Americans and Siberian ancestors," Professor Willersley said. "We have never found something in the fossil record before which very closely resembled Native Americans genetically."

It is thought that the distant ancestors of Native Americans were able to cross from Asia to America (shown as red upper lines in the diagram below) because a land bridge, which some call Beringia, existed from about 34,000 to 11,000 years ago. At that time, sea levels were much lower and hunter gatherers could cross the bridge. They could survive by living on the meat of hairy mammoths and other large animals. Another possible route is around the shore-line, by surviving on plentiful shell-fish and other sea-food in the coastal kelp beds (shown as the blue lower lines below).

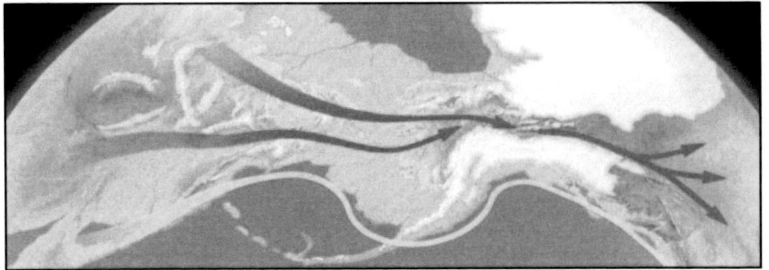

Asian side   Beringia Land bridge   American side

From this start in the far north-west of what is now Alaska, these ancestors then spread south and east to occupy the American continents, North and South, and to found the Native American nations which were there when they met in-coming Europeans.

Not all Native Americans accepted this account of their origins. Although the DNA evidence is strong, some preferred to believe that they have always been there. Some have a story of the origin of their world which refers to a great turtle. This came to the surface with mud on it back, on which the Great Spirit created people from red, white, black and yellow mud. This story is behind the name 'Turtle Island' for the North American Continent. What is important to all is the belief that 'people and the earth are one, all things share the same breath', as Chief Seattle put it.

Just as some Native American Communities will not be celebrating Mayflower 400 in 2020, there is another National holiday in the USA, and other countries of the Americas, which not all Native Americans celebrate. This looks back to the day on which Christopher Columbus 'discovered America', in 1492, over five hundred years ago. Columbus Day is celebrated on the second Monday in October. Many American school children will know the poem:

In fourteen hundred ninety-two
Columbus sailed the ocean blue.
He had three ships and left from Spain;
He sailed through sunshine, wind and rain.
………..
Day after day they looked for land;
They dreamed of trees and rocks and sand.
October 12 their dream came true,
You never saw a happier crew!

"Indians! Indians!" Columbus cried;
His heart was filled with joyful pride.
But "India" the land was not;
It was the Bahamas, and it was hot.

In two States of the USA, Iowa and Nevada, Columbus Day is not celebrated at all. In many US Cities, including Los Angeles, San Francisco and Seattle, the day has been re-designated 'Indigenous Peoples Day'.

It took Christopher Columbus and his three ships, the Santa Maria, the Nina and the La Pinta, ten long weeks before they reached the land which he called 'The New World'. They were hoping to find a new way to the riches of India and Christopher Columbus mistakenly called the people they found 'Indians'.
(by Scarlett M. and Jessica B-H.)

Soon, other nations were sending ships across the ocean to this New World. The Portuguese established settlements in what is now Brazil. The French explored what is now Canada and the Spanish established colonies on both the East Coast of North America in what is now Florida and on the West Coast. Over three centuries, the Spanish expanded their control to establish a New World Empire over vast areas of the Caribbean Islands, half of South America, most of Central America and the areas of today's Mexico, Florida and the Pacific Coastal States of the USA.

Whenever Spanish 'Conquistadors' armed with guns, swords and chain-mail met Native American armies, the Spanish prevailed, until the Empires of the Aztecs in Mexico, the Incas in Peru and the Maya in Guatemala were destroyed. An estimated 1.9 million Spaniards settled in the Americas after 1492 and before the end of the colonial period.

Meanwhile, although English sailors had crossed the Atlantic and had contact with those who lived there, the English, right up to 1607, had failed to establish a permanent foothold in the Americas. Sir Walter Raleigh had tried in 1584, sending men and ships to establish an English colony on Roanoke Island in the Carolinas, but the colony failed.

A sailor from England, who went to the Americas to explore for gold and riches and wanted to remember the experience, wrote about the people in the New World who had very different appearances to them. Some of them wore chains of pearls, some wore necklaces and pendants of bronze found in their land. One of these sailors wrote in his diary, that he didn't see any grey hair on the Native American Indians; they mostly had black hair.

The Native American and the English also had very different lifestyles; to make their clothes, they used the skins from the animals that they had hunted to feast on. Their most important foods were corn on the cob, beans, squash, pumpkins, sweet potatoes, tomatoes, peppers, peanuts and avocados, none of which grew in England at that time. As you can see, they had a very nutritional diet. They grew all their foods and caught lots of fish from the seas.

(by Scarlett M. and Jessica B-H.)

What is less well known is that the English, and other European nations, brought back to Europe not only their stories of exotic foods and different people, but actual men and women from the New World, Native Americans as we would now call them. John White's paintings showed the English what the people of this New World were like and two Native American men were brought

to London, Manteo and Wanchese. Manteo chose to regard himself as a guest of the English, whereas Wanchese thought he was simply a captive. They both lived in the house of Sir Walter Raleigh in London for a time. Manteo and Wanchese must have been very similar to the image of a tall and tattooed Native American chief of the Croatan people in White's picture. It could even have been a portrait of him or of a Croatan chief very like him.

Manteo's story is that of a man who had helped the English as they tried to establish their colony. He became their trusted friend who helped them to survive when their food crops failed, acted as their interpreter and had even learnt some English. When Manteo was in London, he spent time with Thomas Harriot, one of those keen to learn as much as possible about the New World. Harriot learnt some of Manteo's language, Algonquian. Manteo is thought to have returned to Roanoke from London in 1585 and perhaps even went back to England again in 1587. When he returned again to Roanoke with John White, they found that the English who had been left in the colony had disappeared.

Amongst all the exchanges between the English and the Native Americans in the time of Elizabeth I, the links with Manteo stand out as an example of good cultural and race relations. It is in stark contrast to the experience of Native Americans at the hands of the Spanish. The same is true of most of the contact that other Native

Americans had with the English. Apart from the shining examples of Manteo, Pocahontas in early Jamestown and Squanto in the early months of the Plymouth Colony, most of what took place later between the English and the Native Americans they met is best described as mistrust, conflict and open warfare.

3. Pocahontas' Story

When James I became King of England and made peace with Spain a priority, it was not just to end the conflict which had threatened the life and rule of Elizabeth I. It was more to do with opening up the exploration of the Americas and the valuable trade routes in spices, furs, gold and precious stones. Holland had established new ways to financing expensive voyages, especially to the Far East but also to the Americas. The English merchants of London and other cities wanted to share in these developments.

Joint stock companies were set up in which investors could use their wealth to jointly finance a voyage, in the hope that valuable goods would be brought back to their city, and thus generate a good profit on their investment. In London, the Company of Adventurers to New Lands was the first in 1553, followed by the Muscovy Company in 1555, set up to exploit the fur trade with the Russian north. In 1600, the East India Company was chartered to promote trade with India and the Far East. Once peace with Spain had been established and the Atlantic was open again to English ships, the London Virginia Company was established. It was chartered to exploit what were believed to be rich rewards of gold in Virginia, to find a new route through to the Far East and to establish the first permanent English settlement in North America.

The Virginia Company's three ships, the Susan Constant, the Godspeed and the Discovery reached the Capes at the mouth of the Chesapeake Bay on the coast of Virginia on 26th April 1607. The English they carried were not the first Europeans to reach this part of the American coast as a Spanish ship had come into the Chesapeake Bay and had taken some local people captive. They were never seen again.

The area was ruled by a great chief, Powhatan, who had many children, including a girl he called Matoaka. Her mother called her Amonute. Neither name is remembered now because when she was about ten, she was sent back to Powhatan's village to learn the ways of her people and her father gave her a new name, Pocahontas, 'the playful one' or 'the naughty one'. She lived in her Father's village of Tsenacomoco. The remarkable story of Pocahontas is told with the help of pupils at Heacham Middle School, whose book 'Mrs John Rolfe better known as Pocahontas' was published in 2006.

Her childhood was typical of the Algonquin people of the Eastern side of North America and not very different from that of the Wampanoag people further north, but in a much hotter climate.

Amonute's home

Amonute's village was really hot, so hot that little children ran around naked especially in the summer time. The women were very muscular and strong because they had to do all the work. They had to collect water from the river, food from the fields, and prepare animal skins to make clothes, and to make fires. The men had long hair and had to shave the hair from one side of their heads so that when they were shooting arrows their hair would not get caught in their bow strings.

(by Emma from Heacham Middle School)

'Just a normal day'

Men are burning tree trunks into canoes,
Sharpening arrows and spear heads,
Then shooting the arrows at deer, rabbits and turkeys.
Women are skinning the deer for coats,
And making mats for the walls of houses.
Children are practising with bows & arrows.
It's just a normal day in Tsenacomoco.
                    (by Chris R. from Heacham Middle School)

When Amonute was just eleven or twelve, the English came. They set up their fort in the heart of her father's territory, on a low-lying island on the edge of the river the English called the James. Surely Powhatan could have driven the English off their island, but he was interested in these newcomers and allowed them to stay. Soon Pocahontas had befriended the young boys who had come with the English. She also got to know the stocky bearded Captain John Smith, one of the leaders at Jamestown, and taught him some words of her language. He later wrote an account of his time at Jamestown, as they called their fort, and records her delight at doing cartwheels with the English boys down the street at Jamestown.

Algonquian warrior by Rosie

While at Jamestown, Smith took some of the English soldiers to explore the country north of their fort. They got into a fight with the Algonquians and Smith was captured. He later wrote an account of the episode which many believe he made up, but Pocahontas certainly remembered it. He was taken before Powhatan and threatened with execution, when Pocahontas pleaded with her father to save John Smith's life.

Smith claimed that Powhatan not only agreed not to kill him but also made him a member of the Algonquian people. It is certainly true that Smith and Pocahontas, one a tough English soldier in his twenties and the other a young Algonquian girl of twelve, had a close friendship which helped the English to survive when their supplies of grain ran out and they became dependant on trading for corn with the Native Americans.

About two years after reaching Jamestown, Smith nearly died when gunpowder caught fire in his lap. He had to get back to London and he survived, but Pocahontas was told that he had died.

Pocahontas was very sad when she was told that Captain John Smith was dead. All she could think about was her friendship with him. Everybody was comforting her; she was glad that she still had her family and friends around her. Every day she walked far in the forest thinking, talking to herself and singing about her friend Captain John Smith.

(by Helen D. of Heacham Middle School)

Soon she would be a child no longer. She would join the house of the women and begin to cover herself with skirts and cloaks like all the other women of her people. She was given to one of her own, Kocuum, a brave warrior, but there is no record of a child. Perhaps he found the 'Playful One' too disobedient to be a good wife for him. Some believe that he grew tired of her and sent her back to live with her father.

Without strong leadership, the Jamestown Colony struggled to survive. Trade with Powhatan's people for the food they needed to stay alive broke down. It was a time of famine for the Algonquian people too and there was little corn to spare. Soon the English were starving. In the depths of winter 1609-10, they were reduced to digging the bodies of those who had died out of the frozen earth and eating them to survive. Those who have studied Jamestown have found evidence of cannibalism there, not amongst the Native Americans but amongst the English settlers at the fort.

Eventually, new settlers with new leadership arrived from English and the colony was saved. Amongst these newcomers was a young farmer from Norfolk, England, John Rolfe, whose story is for ever linked to Pocahontas. They must have met at Jamestown where Pocahontas was taken when the English captured her and realised that the daughter of Powhatan would be a valuable bargaining chip with her father for the future of the colony. The English captain who kidnapped her claimed that she had come voluntarily, but most believe that she had little choice. Soon both sides were using Pocahontas as a pawn in their attempts to control the other.

Window in Willoughby St Helena's Church

In London, the Virginia Company had promoted a new reason for 'planting' English colonies in America, to establish a 'church of English Christians' there and the conversion of the 'Heathen from the Devil to God' – by which they meant to the Church of England. To this end, Rev. William Whittacker was sent to Jamestown and met the young Algonquian woman known as Pocahontas. She lived in his household.

'The white-skins captured me on June 4th 1613. They wanted to trade me for English prisoners and weapons. But I grew to love being with the English, especially the time spent living with the Reverend. I used to ask him about God and how the world was made. He made me see how wonderful God was, so that while I was there, I wanted to be baptised as a Christian. Every Sunday, I went to church to listen to the Reverend and sing hymns to the glory of God, and it was during one of my visits to church that I first noticed a handsome young man. I discovered that he was called John Rolfe'.

(by Ashleigh E. of Heacham Middle School)

Having met Pocahontas, John Rolfe, who must have been lonely and sad from the loss of his first wife on the voyage from

England, got permission from the Jamestown Governor to marry this Algonquian girl. Any such links between the English and the Algonquian women were strictly forbidden at that time. The Governor gave permission for the union, but first Pocahontas had to be baptised as a Christian.

This window in Willoughby Church depicts the Rev Whittaker dressed as an Anglican priest giving Pocahontas instruction in the Christian faith while they were both at Jamestown.

Pocahontas accepted the faith and was baptised as 'Rebecca' before marrying John Rolfe on April 4th 1614. She was both the first Virginian Native American to accept the Christian faith and the first to marry an Englishman.

21

Rolfe had been experimenting with tobacco varieties to try to find a better leaf than the very rough type grown by the Native Americans around Jamestown. He found a Spanish variety, obtained some seed and successfully grew this tobacco on a farm he established in the area. The 'sweet leaf' he grew and stored in barrels became the main crop produced by the Colony and the foundation of the Virginia tobacco industry. The Virginia Company had at last found a way of making money from their colony and Rolfe and Pocahontas were invited by the Company to travel to London in 1616 with their young son, Thomas.

Even before he had left England as a young man, Rolfe probably took up smoking. Tobacco from Spain and the West Indies was available in England from about 1580, and had been made popular by both Sir Walter Raleigh and Sir Francis Drake. By the early 1600s, people believed that tobacco was an effective cure for many illnesses. It was used as a tincture, ointment, and powder, taken orally as well as smoked. King James I was very much opposed to its use. His 'Counterblaste to Tobacco' was published in 1603 as a royal health warning, describing the smoking of tobacco as

'a custom loathsome to the eye, hateful to the nose, harmful to the brain, dangerous to the lungs, and in the black stinking fume thereof, nearest resembling the horrible Stygian smoke of the pit that is bottomless'.

The royal disapproval seems to have been as ineffective in helping hardened smokers to give up as the current government health warnings. Tobacco smoking was popular in London in the 1600s and the profits from growing it and taking it to Europe were excellent. When John Rolfe, Rebbecca Rolfe, as Pocahontas was now called, their son Thomas, and an escort of Algonquians, sailed for London, they took a cargo of Rolfe's tobacco with them.

It was the first time that any of the Powhatans on the ship had crossed the Atlantic Ocean, although there had been other Algonquian-speaking Indians taken by force across to Europe. When the ship reached Plymouth in June 1616, the Rolfe family went ashore and were taken by coach to London, where the Virginia Company had arranged for the Rolfes to stay at an inn on Ludgate Hill near to the old St Paul's Cathedral. It was called the *'Belle Sauvage'*, and was not the most comfortable of lodgings, but the cost was within the Company's budget. Was the name a coincidence or perhaps it was renamed after Pocahontas's arrival?

Just after the Rolfes reached England, Captain John Smith, who was living in London, published his new book. It was an account of New England, the product of his 1614 voyage to explore the coast of the northern part of what was still called Virginia. He had sailed an open shallop from near to the French colony at Mont Desert Island in the far north to Cape Cod, mapping the whole coastline. On his return to England, Smith had published a map of what he called 'New England'.

When Smith learnt that the Virginia Company proposed to bring Pocahontas to London, he decided to write a letter of introduction on her behalf to Queen Anne. This letter contained the first account of the incident in Powhatan's long-house nine years before, when he claimed that his life had been saved by the great Chief's daughter. Smith described the debt he owed to this Indian Princess and asked the Queen to receive her as a royal visitor. He must have been aware of the Company's plans to use her as a curiosity to help promote the Virginia lottery at minimum cost, cheap lodgings in the city and the paltry sum of £4 a week to pay for all her expenses.

Smith's letter prompted a response. Although the Queen never actually replied, Pocahontas was soon introduced to London society by Lord and Lady Delaware, the former Governor of Virginia and his wife. She was entertained by the Bishop of London, invited to plays and balls and treated with great respect and courtesy. Throughout all this attention, she conducted herself with all the grace and dignity of a Princess. Smith had called her the '*non-pareil*' of her people, an attractive and intelligent young woman, able to adapt to a strange land and trained at Jamestown in the niceties of English etiquette.

While Pocahontas was being entertained by London society, Uttamatomakkin, Powhatan's shaman, was invited to discuss Indian religion with a London vicar, the Rev Samuel Purchas. He was a friend of John Smith and was collecting accounts of life in early Virginia for his book '*Purchas His Pilgrimage or Relations of the World and the Religions observed in all ages and Places discovered from the Creation unto this present*'. It was a project as ambitious as its title was long and Purchas was keen to include an account of Indian religious practice from the most authoritative source, Powhatan's shaman.

Queen Anne, wife of King James I of England and Scotland

In all this social whirl around Pocahontas, John Rolfe seems to have been a spectator. As a commoner and tobacco farmer with no great status, he was not invited to meet King James and Queen Anne, although 'Princess' Pocahontas was. Accompanied by gentry, she went to a Royal Performance of Ben Johnson's 'Vision of Delight' attended by both King and Queen.

Presented formally to the Queen, Pocahontas was impressed by her regal presence. However, when she was required to kneel before the King, she could not believe that the stout, unwashed and scruffy man before her was the great King James in person !

Pocahontas enjoyed her life in London. While she was there, she sat for a portrait by a young Dutch engraver, Simon van de Passe. He had already complete an engraved portrait of Captain John Smith, with the confident bearded face of an experienced soldier. Pocahontas' picture is of a gaunt woman who seems to be much older than her twenty years. She is dressed as a seventeenth century English woman, complete with Prince of Wales feathers in her hand and a high hat.

Copy of the Van der Passe portrait of Pocahontas in the window in Willoughby Church

This is the only image from life of Pocahontas which has survived to our day although there are many other pictures which claim to be of Pocahontas.

Seventeenth century London was a very dangerous place. The plague, tuberculosis, pneumonia and all the diseases we now protect children against, took their toll of young and old alike. Damp houses, smoking chimneys and filthy streets sapped the resistance even of the strong. Those who came from warmer climates with no natural immunity to our diseases were especially vulnerable.

25

Pocahontas was already ill when her portrait was engraved. She was moved with her child out of the city to the cleaner air of Brentford, then a village to the west of London. But even as her health got worse, John Rolfe was impatient to get back to his tobacco farm and to take up his duties as Secretary to the Colony.

Their ship sailed down the River Thames and, off the Kent port of Gravesend, Pocahontas knew that she was dying. She pleaded with Rolfe to be taken ashore. She was carried onto the wharf and they must have found lodgings at a riverside inn. With her husband beside her bed, perhaps holding the two-year-old Thomas in his lap, it was Pocahontas who spoke words of comfort. *'All must die,'* she said, ' *'tis enough that the child liveth.'*

She died in early 1617 and was buried in the chancel of St George's Parish Church, as the register records, although it must have been done in a hurry as the Christian name of the husband is wrong, and her name is given as 'Wroffe', not Rolfe. The chancel tomb within the church was used for the burials of Vicars of the Parish and important local gentry, a fitting place for a Princess who died so far from her own people.

When St George's Church caught fire and burnt down in 1732, the exact place of her burial was lost. The old chancel graves were removed and the remains reburied in a common grave so that the bones of this brave young woman were mixed with all the others buried there and so have been lost. In spite of many attempts to find them in the Gravesend earth, they can never be returned to her people in Virginia.

Nevertheless, this is the place to which many Americans come to pay their respects to the woman whose marriage brought together two peoples, the English and the subjects of Powhatan, her father. Although Pocahontas was no longer there to embody the peace between Powhatan and the English, her influence lived on and peace continued right up to the time of the massacre of the English by the Powhatan in March 1622.

Powhatan's younger brother, Opchanacanough, had decided that the English must be driven out before they occupied all of his lands, as he watched them spread across Virginia and beyond. March 22nd 1622 started like any other day on the tobacco plantations. English and Native Americans went to work in the fields. The Powhatan brought venison and furs to the farmhouses to trade with the English women. But their real plan that day was to use the settlers' own tools and weapons to slaughter the English, killing men, women and children.

The massacre of the English on the James on March 22nd 1622

Reports of this slaughter of English settlers would have reached London not long after the first reports of the English colony at

Plymouth were being received there. When William Bradford wrote in 'Plymouth Plantation' of the 'savage people' that the Pilgrims would be among when they reached America, such reports must have been in his mind:

'...the savage people, who are cruel, barbarous and most treacherous, being most furious in their rage and merciless where they overcome; not being content to only to kill and take away life, but delight to torment men in the most bloody manner that may be; flaying some alive with the shells of fishes, cutting off the members and joints of others by piecemeal and broiling on the coals, eat the collops of the flesh in their sight whilst they live, with other cruelties horrible to be raised.'
(from Chapter III of Plymouth Plantation 1620-1647)

The Native Americans, who had no iron, did use sea-shells to skin their prey and had flayed captive Englishmen alive. They are portrayed as 'savages', but there is no mention in Bradford's writings of those Native Americans who had helped Jamestown to survive, nor of the Native American girl who had come to London with John Rolfe and impressed everyone from the highest in the land to the common people with her grace and ability to adapt to a very different way of life from her own at home in Tsenacomoco, Virginia.

4. Squanto's story

Squanto was thought to have been born around 1585, and was a member of the Native American Patuxet Tribe, living in the area of Cape Cod. Little is known about his early life, but he was taken prisoner by the English, carried across the Atlantic and became a servant in the household of Sir Ferdinando Gorges in Plymouth, England. While there he learned to speak English.
(by Charlie.S, Harlie.H, Olivia.SG, Emily.W and Liam.C)

In 1614, the same year that Pocahontas married John Rolfe at Jamestown, Captain John Smith had sailed back to the American coast to explore the area to the north between 41°N and 45°N.

The French had already established a settlement at Saint Sauveur at the southern edge of their claimed territory of 'Nova Francia'. The English were claiming that Virginia ran right up to this area and had tried to establish a settlement at Sagahadoc at the same time as Jamestown, but it had failed.

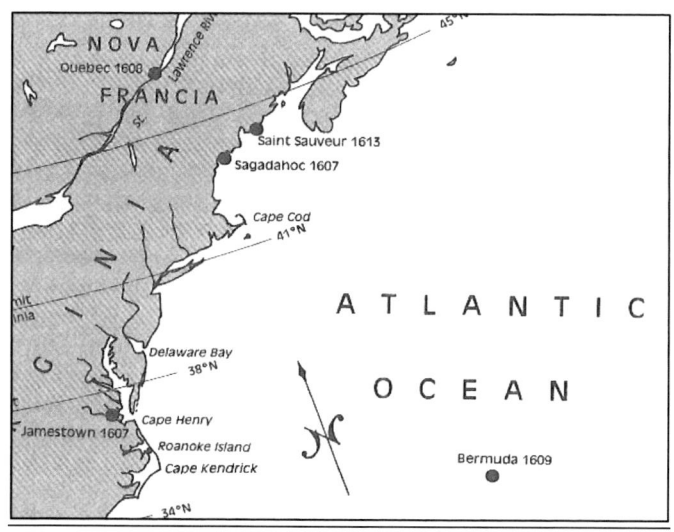

Settlements in North Virginia before the Pilgrims

Smith sailed in an open boat along the coast, from river to river, cape to cape, mapping as he went, and finding out as much as he could from the Native American peoples along the coast. He visited Native American communities along the coast, from what is now the state of Maine to the shores around Cape Cod, the area known as New England. It was Smith who first used this name, and he mapped the area, publishing a map of the coast which was printed in London.

Captain John Smith's Map of the New England coast, with his portrait

Smith, or his advisers, had persuaded Charles, Prince of Wales to act as 'sponsor' for this map and it was Charles who changed the Native American place-names on Smith's original, to his own choice of name. So Cape Cod, which was well known to the English fishing in the region, became Cape James, and the village of Accomack, became 'Plimouth'. Cape Tragabigsanda, which Smith had named after a Turkish lady he knew from an earlier adventure, Charles named after his mother, Anne of Denmark, James' Queen, and this it has remained, as has the Charles River! Smith included in his book a very helpful list of the 'old' and 'new' names:

The old names.	The new names.
Cape *Cod*.	Cape *Iames*.
The Harbor at Cape *Cod*.	*Milforth* hauen.
Chawum.	*Barwick*.
Accomack.	*Plimoth*.
Sagoquas.	*Oxford*.
Massachusets Mount.	*Cheui*[o]*t* hills.
Massachusits Riuer.	*Charles* Riuer.
Totan.	*Fa*[*l*]*mouth*.
A great Bay by Cape *Anne*.	*Bristow*.
Cape *Tragabigsanda*.	Cape *Anne*.
	D t bl

When Captain John Smith visited Gorges in Plymouth and planned his voyage to New England in 1614, he decided to take Squanto with him, intending to leave him in the area of his old home. But while Smith was busy exploring the coast of New England, Captain Hunt, who had been left with Squanto, used him to capture others members of his Patuxet people. They were then all taken to Spain by Hunt and sold as slaves.

In his account of the New England voyage published in 1616, Smith made clear his disappointment in Hunt.

31

"Notwithstanding after my departure, he abused the Savages where he came, and betrayed twenty and seven of these poore innocent soules, which he sold in Spaine for slaves, to move their hate against our Nation, as well as to cause my proceedings to be so much more difficult."

Paula Peters goes on to describe Captain John Smith as *'culturally sensitive and tolerant'* and suggests that his visit to their area just prior to the kidnapping of Squanto and the other Wampanoag *'may have given the Wampanoag a false sense of security. Smith led the 1614 exploration of New England with a primary mission to discover locations suitable to host a colony similar to the one he helped establish in Jamestown'.*

She went on to write, as a member herself of the Wampanoag people; *'If the Jamestown experience with the Powhatan, and having his life spared by Pocahontas, taught Smith anything he certainly understood offenses against the indigenous people to be counter-productive to colonisation. But by the time Smith learned of Hunt's devious act, the Wampanoag were left devastated and Smith's cross-cultural diplomacy squandered.'*

Eventually, Squanto escaped from Spain, got back to England and found a ship sailing to Newfoundland. Once there, one of Gorges' old captains recognised him as 'Sir Ferdinando's Indian'. He took Squanto back to England where, yet again, Gorges sent him back to the New England coast. By that time, Squanto had crossed the Atlantic an extraordinary six times.

When Squanto finally did return to his home, he found that his Patuxet people had been wiped out by diseases introduced by contact with European sailors, against which the Native Americans had no immunity. This is why the Pilgrims found very few people on Cape Cod. They had landed in an area where most of the population had been wiped out. Those that were left had buried their dead on the Cape and then kept well away from any intruders. They had learnt all too clearly that contact could mean death, not from war, but from disease. The graveyard of Squanto's people became the site of Plymouth Plantation.

After he returned home, Squanto had joined the people of Massasoit, the Wampanoag chief of the area, who had another Native American with him who had also leant a little English. One day, as the Pilgrims were building their houses at Plymouth, a tall Native American walked into the settlement and spoke to them in 'broken English'. His name was Samoset. A few days later, he brought more Indians with him and also brought back the tools that had been stolen from Plymouth. Samoset told the English that that the local chief would also visit. His name was Massasoit and he came with an entourage of his people including the Indian called Squanto. Squanto's English was better than Samoset's and for two years, Squanto helped the Pilgrims.

Squanto's real name was Tisquantum and he was married to a woman called Kistapa. He helped the Pilgrims by showing them how to grow crops like corn and he acted as interpreter, between the English and the Native American Wampanoag people. When he fell ill of a fever and lay dying, he asked the Governor, William Bradford, to pray for him so "he could go to the white man's heaven". He died on November 30, 1622 and was buried at Burial Hill Cemetery, Plymouth, Massachusetts. The Pilgrims called him 'a special instrument sent of God for their good'.
(by Charlie.S, Harlie.H, Olivia.SG, Emily.W and Liam.C)

Massasoit, the chief of the Wampanoag people living around Plymouth, agreed a peace treaty with the Plymouth settlement. This provided for *'no injury or hurt'* from one side against the other, for the handing over of any offenders, a mutual defence agreement against common enemies and an agreement that both sides should approach the other unarmed.

Captain John Smith had in fact offered to go with the Pilgrims to be their guide and military leader, but they had declined, preferring to take Miles Standish with them as their military Captain. But the Pilgrims did take with them a copy of John Smith's map, showing the Native American settlement inside Cape Cod as *'Plimouth'* and Plymouth it has remained ever since.

In his later writings, when he knew of the challenges which the Pilgrims had faced in their early months at Plymouth, Smith could not resist saying 'I told you so'! He wrote:

Ignorance caused them, for more than a year, to endure a wonderful deal of misery with an infinite patience; saying my books and maps were much better cheap to teach them than myself....for want of good take-heed (advice)....forty of them died and threescore were left in most miserable estate at New Plymouth where the ship left them......

5. But why did the Mayflower sail?

When the Mayflower sailed from England in 1620, she was carrying two main groups of passengers, those who have become known as the 'saints' and those known as the 'strangers'. Who were these people huddled together in a small sailing ship heading for the New World?

The 'saints' had started thirteen years before when a group of Separatists had left England to travel to Holland. Their religious roots came from a desire to break free from the compulsion to attend Sunday worship, to follow a set service and to accept teaching which many thought was still too close to the Roman

Catholic Church under which so many Protestants had suffered in the time of Queen Mary. Queen Elizabeth had tried to find a middle way, to establish a Church of England which was Protestant but still had some practices which harked back to its Catholic roots. Many in her church accepted this and found the authority of Bishops, the use of a set prayer book and compulsory weekly worship in their parish church quite acceptable. Some wanted to cleanse the church from what they saw as old Papist practices and became known as Puritans.

Others, especially in areas where their clergy had been trained at the most radical Protestant centre at Cambridge, wanted to break free from the national church, to become 'Separatists', to stop attending the Parish Church service altogether and to worship as they wished to. This was of course breaking the law in Elizabethan England where all had to worship in their Parish Church following the Prayer Book.

William Brewster was one of these Separatists. He was born in the Nottinghamshire village of Scrooby, where his father was both postmaster to Queen Elizabeth I and Steward to the Archbishop of York. As a teenager, William was sent to study at Peterhouse, the oldest College of Cambridge University. His first job was as Secretary to William Davison who was in Holland to help the Dutch. Brewster came back to Scrooby and took over his father's role in the village. He got to know a young boy called William Bradford who was an orphan from the nearby village of Austerfield. Together they went to church at Babworth, where Richard Clyfton was Vicar although he did not follow the Bishop's rules about worship. Eventually, Clyfton lost his job and Brewster let his congregation worship in the way they wanted to in his own house at Scrooby. This was against the law at that time, as everyone had to worship using the Prayer Book in their Parish Church.

(by Bella T., Annie P., and Maiteah H.)

Nearby, at Gainsborough Hall, another Separatist group were worshipping and they decided to leave England and move to Holland where they could worship as they wished. They escaped first in 1607.

The Scrooby group decided that they would follow them to Holland, which William Brewster already knew as a place where you weren't told how you had to worship. You could worship the way you liked. They first tried to escape from Boston in 1607, but their captain betrayed them and they were arrested. They eventually managed to escape from the Lincolnshire coast at Immingham, but their women and children got left behind on the shore and had to join them later. They all got to settle in the Dutch city of Leiden, but after years living there, their children were losing their English and religious distinctiveness. The parents, including Brewster, decided they would have to leave again.

(by Scarlett M and Max P.)

The tolerant Protestant Dutch had allowed them to worship as they wished and they could have stayed there permanently. Brewster established a printing business and they settled into life in Leiden with their families. But having decided to leave, they planned this time to start a completely new settlement in the wilderness of America.

Englishmen who wished to establish a new settlement in Virginia could only do so by getting the agreement of the Virginia Company and this could only be done through an agent in London. The Scrooby Separatists, now a distinct Leiden Church group with two lay Deacons, John Carver and Robert Cushman, and an ordained pastor, the Rev. John Robinson, sent Carver and Cushman to London to negotiate on their behalf with the Council of the Virginia Company and its most influential leader, Sir Edwin Sandys. He was known to be sympathetic to Puritans and was keen to recruit more colonists for Virginia.

Robinson and Brewster had sent a letter to the Council of the London Virginia Company carried by John Carver and Robert Cushman. Strictly speaking, the London Company could only give approval for a settlement as far north as Manhattan Island but this might be far enough. Although the area which John Smith's map called New England was further north, there was plenty of space between Jamestown and Manhattan.

Carver and Cushman got an encouraging response from Sandys and the Council of the Virginia Company but there was a problem, the matter of religion. If the Leiden church could agree to become loyal members of the Church of England, or the King's Church' as they called it, it would be relatively easy to get permission to settle in Virginia. But the Leiden church would not compromise on matters of religion. They had escaped from the 'King's Church' and had no wish to go back.

If they admitted to being 'Separatists', the King and his advisers were hardly likely to approve their settlement in an area which was still directly under the King's authority. So Brewster and Robinson sent a series of carefully worded letters to Sandys and the Council. Eventually, the Council of the Virginia Company agreed to their request. Their good reputation with the Dutch, who both admired their hard work and respected their honesty, helped them. Members of the Council spoke up for them when the matter was considered by the King and emphasised that they would try to both spread the Gospel and extend English influence in the New World. When he asked how they proposed to support themselves, an inspired response 'by fishing', won King James' approval. 'Fishing' said the King, 'so God have my soul, 'tis an honest trade; 'twas the Apostles' own calling.'

Eventually, Robinson and Brewster agreed to appear to accept much of what the King and the Bishops demanded, without actually saying so. By the time they were 3,000 miles away, on the other side of the Atlantic, they would be free to follow their own consciences without much interference from England. As Bradford put it, '*they presumed they should not be troubled*'. Wisely keeping Brewster's name out of their submission, they were granted a 'patent' to settle in Virginia, dated June 9th 1619 in the name of John Wincop, who worked for Elizabeth Clinton Fynnes, the Countess of Lincoln. The way to America seemed to be clear.

As they always did when considering an important decision, the Leiden church came together for a '*solemn meeting and day of humiliation*' led by Pastor Robinson with sermons and prayers. They decided to go, in spite of all the difficulties. But they also decided to divide into two groups. About half of the church would leave with their Ruling Elder, William Brewster, and sail to Virginia. Some would remain in Leiden with their Pastor and ordained Minister, John Robinson. They all knew each other well so those who stayed would look after some of the children of those who went. At some later date, Robinson and those remaining in Leiden would join the others in the New World.

The group leaving for America would have no ordained minister until Robinson could join them, as Brewster had never been ordained. For however long it took, he would be solely responsible for preaching, teaching and leading their acts of worship. Without Robinson, they would not be able to celebrate the sacrament of Communion.

There were other more practical matters to attend to. They soon realised that their finances would not cover the full cost of such a venture and they needed more people.

They knew that they had to get enough people to form a permanent settlement because half of them would probably die before the end of the first year. That is what had happened to the settlement at Jamestown. These extra people would be encouraged to join them and most came from the London area. Because those coming from Leiden were all members of the Separatist Church there, they were called 'Saints'. They did not know any of the extra people who joined from London and these were called 'Strangers'. The Saints bought an old ship called the Speedwell and sailed her over to Southampton, where they were joined by the Strangers sailing from London in the ship called the Mayflower.

(by Scarlett M. and Max P.)

The Leiden group agreed to invite a London Merchant called Weston to help them by setting up a joint-stock company to raise the extra finance they needed. Rich people in London, called the Adventurers would buy shares in the new colony as a joint stock company, just as the investors in the Jamestown venture had done. Early profits would not come from finding gold but from the rich fishing and fur-trading which was already bringing a return to wise investors in American ventures, or so Weston promised them. They would get a patent from the Virginia Company by applying as Adventurers making no mention of the Pilgrims and their religious commitment.

The Leiden church agreed to join forces with Weston's 'Adventurers' because they thought the terms were reasonable. Weston promptly changed these to their disadvantage. They would have to work more days per week for the company, up from five to seven, and have to wait seven years before they would have their own land. Carver and Cushman, as the Leiden church representatives, reluctantly agreed to this because the majority were already so heavily committed to leaving Holland that they had little choice. The arrangements descended further into chaos when another agent claiming to be acting for them started to buy up provisions for the voyage without consulting Carver. It was not a good start for such a risky venture.

6. Becoming Pilgrims

They had started from Scrooby and became known as the Scrooby Separatists. They spent nearly twelve years in Leiden and became the Leiden church. Writing much later, William Bradford gave them the new name by which they are known today, in his account of their departure from Holland.

'They knew they were pilgrims, and looked not much on those things, but lifted up their eyes to the heavens, their dearest country, and quietened their spirits.'

But first they had to get to England to link up with those who had been recruited by the Adventurers mainly from the London area. Just where William Brewster was at this time is something of a mystery. He was still in hiding, either in Leiderdorp just outside Leiden, or somewhere in England.

None of them knew anything about ships and the Speedwell turned out to be a very poor buy. The suspicion is that the Speedwell's Captain never intended to sail the Atlantic in her, knowing that she would not make it. He also replaced her masts at their expense, a change which was to prove disastrous when she met the heavy winds of the Channel, let alone the open ocean. They also decided to recruit a soldier whom Robinson trusted, Miles Standish, to be responsible for their defences when they reached Virginia. They did not believe that the Native Americans would receive them in peace and Standish was an experienced veteran of the campaigns against the Spanish.

The group who were leaving distributed the things they did not think they would need amongst their friends in Leiden. Those of their families who were staying in Leiden found new homes. William Brewster and his wife decided to take ten year old, Love, and their youngest, six year old, Wrestling, with them, but left Jonathan to continue to work in Leiden. Patience and Fear stayed too, with the Robinson family. As William had requested, Mary also packed all the books in William's library to take with them, no doubt grumbling as wives do about their husbands' priorities. William and Mary Bradford left their only son, John, then just six years old, in Leiden with friends.

In July 1620, after a service and supper, the whole church, and even some of their friends from Amsterdam, helped those who were going to load their belongings into a canal boat on the Rhine running through Leiden. Together, they set off south, passing through the city of Delft to the point where the Rhine canal joined the estuary of the Maas, at Delftshaven, where the *Speedwell* was waiting for them. With John Robinson's farewell prayer ringing in their ears, they went aboard, *'the tide, which stays for no man, calling them away'*. A *'prosperous wind'* took them swiftly across the Channel to Southampton, where Carver, Cushman, Weston and the Strangers were waiting for them in the larger ship, the *Mayflower.* William Brewster came out of hiding and slipped on board.

At Southampton, the arguments continued, with Weston demanding that the Pilgrims agree to the new terms. When they refused, Weston withdrew all further financial help and the Pilgrims had to sell some of their supplies to pay for the work that had been done on the *Speedwell.* As they had more butter than they needed, thanks to the confusion over who was supposed to be buying what, this was not too much of a hardship. On August 5th, they sailed at last, the *Speedwell* carrying most of the Pilgrims and the *Mayflower* with the Strangers. Just before they left, a letter from John Robinson was read, encouraging them to establish a proper system of government, so they chose Christopher Martin to lead those on the *Mayflower* and their Deacon, Robert Cushman, those on the *Speedwell.*

Out in the Channel, the *Speedwell* soon began to leak. Her new masts put too much strain on the hull and they had to put in to the port of Dartmouth for more repairs, and yet more expense. When they tried again, even before they reached Land's End, the leaking *Speedwell* began to fill up.

Mayflower II, the full scale replica ship now moored
at Plymouth, Massachusetts

Hastily returning to the safety of Plymouth, they were faced with a decision. Although the *Mayflower* was really only large enough to take the Strangers, they could not go without the Saints. Some of the Strangers gave up the idea of going to Virginia and left. Transferring their belongings to the hold of the larger ship, the Saints joined the already crowded Strangers to the tight space on the *Mayflower's* gun deck. There were now seventy men and women and thirty-two children in a space about seventy feet long and twelve feet wide, a space not much bigger that our classroom at school.

Each family had the use of one of these spaces on the Mayflower's gun deck

At last they were ready to leave Plymouth, on September 6th 1620. The first few days of their voyage were calm and peaceful and the two groups, most of whom had never met each other before could at last get to know each other. They were very different. The Saints had been living and worshipping together for years and shared a conviction that the God who had brought them out of England would ensure that they reached their 'promised land' of America. Their fellow passengers, the Strangers, were a mixed bag of English men and women, with no more than the general interest in religion that everyone in Seventeenth Century England had. Some hoped to make their fortunes in America, some were hired hands brought along as servants. Now they were all flung together to form one group, which Brewster had said were 'Pilgrims'.

Captain Christopher Jones' crew were as tough a bunch of seamen as you would find on any ship. They had no sympathy for the soft passengers unused to such rough conditions and openly mocked them. One of the younger seamen was particularly abusive and told them all that they would die at sea and find a watery grave. When he was the first to become ill and died '*in a desperate manner and so was the first that was thrown overboard*', the Pilgrims believed that his profanity had been punished by God Himself.

In the sixty five days that it took the Mayflower to reach the North American coast, he was the only person on board to die. But the ship was blown off course and in the middle of the Ocean, a big storm hit the ship. Passengers and crew were terrified that the Mayflower would sink and they would all drown. Somehow, they managed to stop the ship from breaking up and eventually the storm eased.

They started with 32 children and on the voyage, somewhere in the middle of the Atlantic, there were 33. The wife of Stephen Hopkins gave birth to a baby boy, in that crowded ship. They called him Oceanus and both mother and child survived. They were both still alive when the Mayflower eventually reached the American coast. (by Bella T.)

They had planned to settle in what is now the Manhattan region around New York, but in November 1620, the Pilgrims recognised their first sight of land. It was the strange curved spit which was shown on John Smith's map as Cape James, but which sailors knew as Cape Cod. For a time, they tried to sail south, but found that the shoals along the Coast were so dangerous that Christopher Jones took his ship round the head of the Cape and into the calm waters of a safe harbour. They moored near to the point where Provincetown now lies.

Before they went ashore, William Brewster and William Bradford called the grown-up men together, both Saints and Strangers, to sign an agreement between all of them, as to how they were going to organise themselves. It is called 'The Mayflower Compact' setting out the principles on which they would base their new community. We still have a copy of it today.

(by Annie P.)

The Mayflower Compact

In the name of God, Amen. We, whose names are underwritten, the Loyal Subjects of our dread Sovereign Lord, King James, by the Grace of God, of England, France and Ireland, King, Defender of the Faith, e&. Having undertaken for the Glory of God, and Advancement of the Christian Faith, and the Honour of our King and Country, a voyage to plant the first colony in the northern parts of Virginia; do by these presents, solemnly and mutually in the Presence of God and one of another, covenant and combine ourselves together into a civil Body Politick, for our better Ordering and Preservation, and Furtherance of the Ends aforesaid; And by Virtue hereof to enact, constitute, and frame, such just and equal Laws, Ordinances, Acts, Constitutions and Offices, from time to time, as shall be thought most meet and convenient for the General good of the Colony; unto which we promise all due submission and obedience. In Witness whereof we have hereunto subscribed our names at Cape Cod the eleventh of November, in the Reign of our Sovereign Lord, King James of England, France and Ireland, the eighteenth, and of Scotland the fifty-fourth. Anno Domini, 1620. (There followed the forty one signatures of the male adult Pilgrims on the Mayflower, at anchor in Providence Bay, Cape Cod.)

They chose one of the Pilgrims, John Carver, to be their first Governor, and planned to explore their new surroundings around Cape Cod Bay. Stored in sections on the Mayflower was a 'shallop', an open boat in which they could row or sail from the ship into the shallow waters along the shore. Assembling the boat, and making her watertight took time and energy but they were soon ready. They found a sandy shore with shallow rivers running into the sea, not unlike the coast of Lincolnshire they had first left and the Dutch coast west of Leiden, and they began the long hard process of establishing a new community.

7. Stephen Hopkins' story

Seventy men and women and thirty two children passengers had set out from Plymouth on the Mayflower, but when they reached Cape Cod, there were thirty three children. A baby was born in mid-Atlantic to Mrs Stephen Hopkins, the wife of one of the Strangers. It is hard enough to imagine what conditions must have been like on the Mayflower gun-deck with some many families crammed in. It is almost impossible to imagine what it must have been like for Elizabeth to give birth in that situation in mid-ocean. She would have had the help of the other women, but no doctor, no medical facilities and with her own family already occupying their tiny space, Stephen and Elizabeth, his teenage children by his first wife, Constance and Giles, his son by Elizabeth, Damaris, and now a baby, they were all there. They christened the baby Oceanus and he did survive the voyage, so one hundred and three reached America.

There are three contemporary accounts of what happened in the early years of Plymouth Plantation which have survived from the 1620s. William Bradford's account, probably written some years later, from which we have already quoted. *'Mourt's Relation'* – a journal of the Pilgrims at Plymouth, probably written by Edward Winslow with some input from Bradford, which covers the period up to December 1621, and the account written by Edward Winslow himself, titled *'Good News from New England'*, published in London in 1624, which covers December 1621 to September 1623. The best account of the first weeks that the Pilgrims spent in the New World are in Mort's Relations, and it is that source that we have used for this account of exploring Cape Cod.

The Pilgrims decided to explore the area as soon as they could and used their shallop to send a party of sixteen men from the Mayflower at anchor to reach the shore. They were very cautious, fully armed with muskets and swords and under the command of Captain Miles Standish. William Bradford, Stephen Hopkins and Edward Tilley led the party inland following tracks which they thought had been made by Native Americans. Having camped overnight, they came across a cultivated area and found an old ruined 'house' and a 'great kettle' which they thought must have come from a European ship visiting the area. There appeared to be a mound which covered a 'little old basket full of fair Indian corn'. Digging further, they found a 'fine great new basket full of very fair corn of this year'.

'The basket was round and narrow at the top; it held about three or four bushels, which was as much as two of us could lift up from the ground and was very handsomely and cunningly made. But whilst we were busy about these things, we set our men sentinel in a round ring, all but two or three which digged up the corn.'

(Mourt's Relations, p22)

This was the first Native American food found by the Pilgrims and they were uncertain about simply taking it for themselves. They decided that they would take both the kettle and as much corn as they would carry, but agreed that should they meet the rightful owners, they would offer some compensation.

' ...if we could find any of the people, and come to parley with them, we would give them the kettle again and satisfy them for their corn. So we took all the ears and put a good deal of the loose corn in the kettle, for two men to bring away on a staff; besides, they that could put any into their pockets filled the same. The rest we buried

again, for we were so laden with armour that we could carry no more.' *(Mourt's Relations)*

After finding an old fort, evidence that the Spanish or the French had been there before them, they found a river and on the banks, two canoes. They spent a very wet night camping by a pond, keeping careful watch and set off again in the morning to explore further.

'As we wandered, we came to a tree, where a young sprit (sapling) *was bowed down over a bow, and some acorns strewed underneath. Stephen Hopkins said it had been to catch some deer. So as we were looking at it, William Bradford being in the rear, when he came looked also upon it, and as he went about, it gave a sudden jerk up, and he was immediately caught by the leg. It was a very pretty device, made with a rope of their own making and having a noose as artfully made as any roper in England can make, and as like ours as can be, which we brought away with us.'* *(Mourt's Relations)*

This is the first mention in any of the accounts that one of them, out of all the men on the Mayflower, had actually been to the New World before, Stephen Hopkins. He recognised the trap which had whisked William Bradford into the air as the same device that he had seen used by Native Americans at Jamestown. He alone out of the Pilgrims had been to America before and his experience would prove invaluable to the Pilgrims. So how did he get involved in the Mayflower voyage?

Stephen Hopkins was born in the small Hampshire village of Clatford All Saints, which lies just south of the town of Andover, on the banks of the River Anton. He was baptised in the parish church of All Saints which still stands in the water-meadows beside the river. The date in the baptismal register is 13th April 1581.

His father was a farmer, working land at Normans Court in the village. When Stephen was about five, the family moved to the city of Winchester where his father died when Stephen must have been about twelve. He does not reappear in the records again until his first child, Elizabeth, was baptised in the parish church of Hursley, a village to the north west of Winchester. The register records Mary Hopkins as the mother, so she and Stephen were probably married a year or two before 1605, the baptismal date. A second daughter, Constance, was baptised in the same church, and their first son, Giles, in 1609.

Stephen was, like Captain John Smith of Jamestown, the son of a tenant farmer, and he went on to become a tenant farmer himself, with a lease for land at Merton Manor in the parish of Hursley. But his farming lease ran out and he needed to find another way of supporting his growing family. He must have moved to London, leaving Mary and the children in Hampshire to support themselves. Some believe that she became a shop-keeper but there is no record of this apart from the list of shop-fittings which appears in the inventory of her possessions at her death.

Stephen reached London just as the Virginia Company were recruiting men to join a new fleet sailing to Jamestown. The flagship was to be the Sea Venture, captained by Christopher Newport, who had taken the first fleet to Jamestown in 1607 and the Company published an attractive poster to tempt potential colonists into joining the voyage. Stephen Hopkins may have seen the poster when he reached London or he could have seen it in Winchester. The Virginia Company had strong links with his part of Hampshire as Sir Thomas West, a member of the Council, was born at Wherwell, the village just next to Clatford, and was roughly Stephen's contemporary. He became the 3rd Baron De La Ware. Although from a very different level of Elizabethan society, Stephen and Sir Thomas may well have had people who knew both, like Sir Thomas' servants.

What the poster below does not show is that the Sea Venture, the ship depicted, was new and not yet tested at sea. When used for the Virginia voyage, the ship's caulking, the packing of the seams to make her water-tight, was loose and she leaked badly. That was bad enough, but the real disaster was when the fleet was struck by a hurricane north of the Caribbean. The Sea Venture was driven north onto the rocks of what are now the Bermuda islands. They were called the Devil's Islands at the time because of the multiple shipwrecks.

LXVIII.

NOVA BRITANNIA.

OFFRING MOST

Excellent fruites by Planting in

VIRGINIA

Exciting all fuch as be well affeƈted
to further the fame.

LONDON
Printed for SAMVEL MACHAM, and are to be fold at
his Shop in Pauls Church-yard, at the
Signe of the Bul-head.
1 6 0 9.

The Sea Venture carried all the new leaders of Jamestown, Admiral George Somers, Vice-Admiral Christopher Newport, the new governor for the Virginia Colony, Sir Thomas Gates, and William Strachey, who wrote an account of the wreck which was sent back to London. She also carried a Norfolk farmer, John Rolfe, with his pregnant wife and with them on board was Stephen Hopkins. He had been appointed Minister's Clerk to the new Chaplain for Jamestown, the Rev. Richard Buck. How farmer Stephen got this role is not clear but he must have had at least enough education to be able to read the Psalms and make the appropriate responses during services in support of the Minister.

The hurricane lasted three days and the ships were separated. Admiral Somers steered the Sea Venture into a cleft in an island reef to stop her sinking. Held in the rocks, this saved everyone on board, one hundred and fifty men and women and several dogs, but the ship was destroyed. The islands were named 'The Somers Isles' after Admiral Somers, although they also became known as the Bermudas. The survivors lived on Bermuda for a time and built two smaller vessels from salvaged parts of the *Sea Venture,* which they named *Deliverance* and *Patience. T*en months later, they sailed on to Jamestown, arriving at Jamestown on 23 May 1610.

Stephen Hopkins had got into trouble while on Bermuda by wanting to stay there when the plan to sail on to Jamestown was made. There was plenty of fresh fruit and fish to eat on the island. There was pork from the pigs from previous ship-wrecks and the climate was good. He was charged with mutiny and sentenced to hang, much as John Smith had been sentenced for being insubordinate on his voyage to Virginia, but both were reprieved. Hopkins pleaded for his life on the grounds that he had a wife and children to support at home in England, dependants he appears to have abandoned to join the voyage!

When their two small ships reached Jamestown, they found that most of the five hundred English who had been sent there had died during what became known as the 'Starving Time'. The *Sea*

Venture passengers had hoped to find a thriving colony at Jamestown and had brought little food or supplies with them. The reality of the mess at Jamestown led them to turn round to sail on home, but the Jamestown colony was saved. A supply mission headed by Thomas West, 3rd Baron De La Warr, who became known as 'Lord Delaware', arrived just as they were abandoning the colony. West had been appointed as Governor General for life to replace the governing council of the colony, and he had recruited and equipped a new supply convoy at his own expense, sailing from England in March 1610. He had the distinction of having a river, a State of the USA and a nation of Native Americans, all named after him.

While he was at Jamestown, as the Minister's Clerk, Stephen Hopkins would have been involved in most of the church services at Jamestown. He would have witnessed the ceremonies when Pocahontas was baptised as Rebecca, and when she was married to John Rolfe. He would have learnt a lot about the way the Native Americans hunted, grew their food and organised their society. He may well have entertained some in his house and even learnt a few words of their Algonquin language. As the only man on board the Mayflower who had this invaluable experience, it is hardly surprising that those who recruited the 'Strangers' in London decided to take him on board.

It must have been in 1613 or 1614, when the Virginia Company in London sent a message to Jamestown to tell Stephen that his wife, Mary, had died. He was their employee and she had probably been receiving some of the earnings due to him from the Company. It was agreed that he should be sent back to London on the next available ship. He could even have sailed on the ship which took John Rolfe, Pocahontas and their infant son, Thomas back to England. When Stephen reached London, some time around 1616, he must have been reunited with at least two of his children, Constance and Giles, but Elizabeth, his older daughter, is not mentioned again in any of the records.

Stephen met and married his second wife, Elizabeth Fisher, in London in 1618 and a year later their first child was born and baptised, a girl they named Damaris. The couple were living in the parish of St Mary's, Whitechapel, in East London, the neighbouring parish to the home of Thomas Weston, the Merchant Adventurer who had become the agent for the Leyden Church in London and had recruited investors and adventurers to make their venture of leaving England financially possible.

There is no record of when and how Hopkins first heard of the Leyden church's plans, but he must have found the terms which Weston was offering very attractive. Passages to Virginia were offered to anyone who would exchange seven years of labour in the new settlement for one share in the proposed joint-stock company. No cash investment was needed, just an undertaking to work. Children were welcomed. If they were between ten and sixteen like Giles and Constance, they would each receive half a share; those under ten, like Damaris, would receive a token land grant of fifty acres.

Basic needs such as food, clothing and housing would be provided by the Company, using the labour of those who became colonists. Profits would come from timber, furs, fishing and trade with Native Americans. At the end of seven years, the Company would be wound up and each shareholder get, it was hoped, a substantial return and their share of all the assets, including land and houses.

With his wife and children joining him, Stephen would become a significant holder of Company shares, to a total value of £30. He could also increase this still further by taking two young men with him as servants, Edward Doty and Edward Leister. Each would add a further share. By taking his whole household to Virginia, Stephen Hopkins could become a significant investor in the new Company and a significant land-holder if he survived his seven years of service.

Stephen and Elizabeth and their household probably joined the Mayflower when Captain Christopher Jones welcomed the Strangers on board at Rotherhithe on the south bank of the Thames in London. They must have sailed with them around the coast to the port of Southampton where they met with the Speedwell carrying the Saints from Leiden. On August 4th, the two ships sailed together from Southampton but they had to put into the Devon port of Dartmouth to attend to the leaks in the Speedwell. They tried again but got no further than Lands' End at the edge of the Atlantic, when their Captains decided to return to the safety of Plymouth harbour.

Those who decided to continue on the Mayflower in spite of the delays then had to find space for the Saints to join them, as the Speedwell was left at Plymouth. Finally, the Mayflower sailed on September 6th 1620.

There is no record of the conversations which Stephen may have had with the other passengers over the long days and nights as they were tossed about by Atlantic gales. The birth of his son, Oceanus, is recorded but he must have told the other passengers about his time in Jamestown and they must have asked him about his shipwreck, his journey to Jamestown, his three or four years in the colony and most important, his knowledge of the Native Americans he had met, including Pocahontas

There were in fact two members of the Mayflower's crew who had been to Jamestown. The Master's Mate, John Clark had been there in 1611, when Hopkins was also there. He had been kidnapped by a Spanish ship, held in Havana in what is now Cuba and taken to Madrid before being released in a prisoner exchange. Clark had been back to Jamestown a second time, in 1618, on a supply ship to the colony. But none of the other passengers, Saints or Strangers, had ever been across the Atlantic before.

The actual ocean crossing took sixty five days, but the Hopkins family, and the others who had come on board the Mayflower as Strangers from London, had been in her cramped gun deck from

July 1620. One hundred and fifty days later, in December 1620, they were still there, moored in the shelter of Provincetown harbour, sheltered by the ship, but no nearer to establishing a new home in the New World.

The decision was made to establish their new settlement on the site of the Wampanoag Native American village of *Accomac,* renamed by Prince Charles and marked as *Plimouth* on John Smith's map. At last, those who were still fit to work could start to build the houses which they desperately needed, as the New England winter began to bite. Until they had houses, the women and children had to stay on board the Mayflower, but at least they were sheltered by her hull.

Taking over a site that had been a Wampanoag settlement meant that it was at least already cleared of trees. But the Pilgrims had to fell more trees from which to build their houses, back breaking-work for fit young men, but exhausting for the older Pilgrims and those already weakened by scurvy as most were. Bad weather stopped them from working on December 21st and 22nd, but on the 23rd, they started to fell trees and collect the timber on the building site. The first house-frame went up on Christmas Day, which the Pilgrims did not celebrate as a special day, and it was not until two weeks later that the structure was finished, a 'common house' twenty foot by twenty foot, with wattle and daub walls and tiny windows of parchment water-proofed with linseed oil.

On a neighbouring hill, they built a timber platform for the gun they brought from the Mayflower, and between these first two structures, they laid out a settlement of two rows of houses, nineteen in all, to house all the families, with single men living with whoever would share their house with them. The plan was that each household would build their own house, but there were many in the settlement too weak to work and soon the number of houses was reduced to just seven.

8. The Seasoning and the Great Dying

The Pilgrims had already lost one woman before they first came ashore at what is now 'Plymouth Rock'. William Bradford's young wife Mary had slipped over the side of the Mayflower and drowned in the sea. One of the children left in the care of the Brewster family, seven-year old Jasper More, died on the day before and his brother and his sister would die in the next few months. Weakened by months on the Mayflower, surviving on a meagre diet of salt pork and ship's biscuit, with very little Vitamin C, most of the Pilgrims were already weak with scurvy when they first came ashore.

Of the first one hundred settlers who reached Jamestown in 1607, sixty would be dead within six months. Some were killed by the Powhatan, and some died in accidents, but the great majority died from disease. They were exposed to new pathogens and a new climate on a low-lying island plagued by insects with a poor water-supply. When new colonists came to join the remnants of those already there, the death-rate from these factors remained high, even if it would be small compared to the casualties of starvation when food supplies for the colonists ran out. This initial dying-off of colonists within the first six months of their arrival was referred to by the English as 'the Seasoning'. It was regarded as an inevitable consequence of any attempt to plant a colony on an unfamiliar shore. As Christopher Newport welcomed his passengers onto the Sea Venture in 1609, he must have known that half of them would be dead before the year was out.

At Plymouth Plantation, the Pilgrims, once ashore, needed all the able-bodied to help with felling timber before they could start building. They could still use the Mayflower for overnight shelter and they decided where to build and allocated plots according to the numbers in each family. They had steel axes for the felling, which the Native Americans lacked, as they had no iron and were effectively a stone-axe using culture.

56

John White had brought back images of the way Native Americans could fell a tree and make a canoe from the trunk. These images were then turned into engravings (left) so that they could be printed to illustrate a book about the New World. They used bark-ringing to kill the tree, a passing hurricane to fell it and fire and sea-shells to open out a log into the shape of a dug-out canoe. Much the same methods were used by the Wampanoag in the Plymouth area and at Plimouth Plantation today there is a demonstration (right) of their techniques staffed by members of the Wampanoag community.

Even though they had steel axes, the very hard work of felling timber and building houses exhausted the Pilgrims. Soon very few were left who could still work and they were needed to care for the others. William Bradford recorded this hard time:

'But that which was most sad and lamentable was, that in two or three months' time, half of the company died, especially in January or February, being the depth of winter, and wanting

homes and other comforts; being infected with the scurvy and other diseases which this long voyage and their inaccommodate conditions had brought upon them. There died sometimes three or four of a day in the foresaid time, so that of one hundred and odd persons, scare fifty remained. And of these, in the time of most distress, there were but six or seven sound persons who to their great commendations, be it spoken, spare no pains night and day, but with the abundance of toil and hazard of their own health fetched water, made them fires, dressed them meat, made their beds, washed their loathsome clothes, clothed and unclothed them. In a word, did all the homely and necessary offices for them which dainty and queasy stomachs cannot endure to be named; and all this willingly and cheerfully, ...showing their true love unto their friends and brethren...'

(William Bradford 'Of Plymouth Plantation' Chapter X1)

Of the 103 passengers who reached Cape Cod, four died before she moored off Plymouth. By the summer of 1621, fifty had died. Only twelve of the original twenty six heads of families and four of the original single men and boys were left. Of the eighteen women who boarded Mayflower in England, three of whom were already pregnant, just five were still alive at the end of their first hard winter in America. The 'Seasoning' had struck the Pilgrims even more savagely that it struck the first settlers of Jamestown.

Amongst the survivors were the family and servants of Stephen Hopkins. Perhaps his previous experience in Jamestown helped him and those close to him to get through. Whatever the reason, Stephen, his wife Elizabeth, their older children Constance, Giles and Damaris, and even the baby, Oceanus, were all still alive, and their two servants, Edward Doty and Edward Leister had also survived.

When building work resumed, the Hopkins household was one of the few that managed to complete their new home and thatch it with the grass around the settlement. It was certainly complete by the time the next contact with Native Americans took place, for the

Pilgrims had yet to meet any significant numbers of Native Americans. All around them was evidence that people had lived there. They had found graves of adults and of children, abandoned houses and areas that had been cleared of the original forest. But they met no people. It seemed that the Native Americans were shunning these incomers, avoiding any contact with them.

What they did not know, was that their fear of the Native Americans as 'savages', was matched by these people's fear of dying from disease.

'Europeans brought many diseases such as: smallpox (caused by a virus called Variola), measles (a contagious infectious disease), diphtheria (that can cause heart failure and even death) chickenpox (it can cause skin rashes), scarlet fever (a fever that causes bad rashes and death) and many more. The Native Americans had no protection against these diseases because of their lack of contact with them before. The most destructive disease by far was the smallpox. The Lakota Indians called the disease 'the running face sickness'.

The loss of many people from disease meant that the tribes shrunk. As the groups of people died, there were less people to hunt, plant crops and it was a lot harder for the living humans to live. There was more chance of even more people dying. The Native Americans called this time 'the Great Dying'.
(by Toby.B, Rio.M, Jasmine.M, Monet.P, Liam.S and Jamie.W)

For the Wampanoag people who had lived in the area around the Pilgrim settlement, the death rate was catastrophic. When Squanto returned to his Patuxet home in 1619, he is said to have found that all his people had died. Which disease caused this wiping-out of the Wampanoag in the years 1616-19 is not generally agreed but there is evidence that it may have been leptospirosis. 90% of a population estimated at 20-25,000 people had died. It is no wonder that the Wampanoag who survived and their neighbouring tribes were extremely cautious of any further contact with European interlopers.

It was not until February 17th that any close contact was made. Two men appeared on a neighbouring hill and gestured to the English for them to approach. Mile Standish and Stephen Hopkins went across to meet them but the Native Americans ran off. Four days later, Captain Jones organised the transfer of Mayflower's gun to the timber platform at the end of the Plymouth street, and on March 16th, they had another visitor. To the great surprise of the English, this man 'saluted' them and said 'Welcome, Englishmen'!

He introduced himself as Samuset, a tall man armed with a bow and two arrows, but with no clothes. He asked them for beer, but they gave him 'strong water' and some of their food to eat. He explained that he was a sachem from the area to the north, what is now Maine, and he had learnt some English from fishermen who were frequently in that area. He wanted to stay at Plymouth overnight so they agreed he should join Stephen Hopkins' family in their house, before leaving in the morning. He promised to return and to bring with him a man from that area whose English was better than his.

They came on March 22nd, Samuset and four other Native Americans, one of whom was Squanto, who was soon talking fluently to the English in their own language to their great surprise. He had been in London, as well as Spain and Newfoundland. He and Samuset explained that Massasoit, the Wampanoag sachem or Chief and his brother were nearby and wished to speak to them.

The Pilgrims described Massasoit as *'a very lusty man, in his best years, an able body, grave of countenance, and spare of speech. In his attire, little or nothing differing from the rest of his followers, only in a great chain of white bone beads about his neck, and behind his neck hangs a little bag of tobacco, which he drank and gave us to drink; his face was painted with a sad red like murry, and oiled both head and face, that he looked greasily. All his followers likewise, were in their faces, in part or in whole painted, some black, some red, some yellow and some white, some with crosses, and other antic works; some had skins on them, and some naked, all strong, tall, all men in their appearance.'*

(from Mourt's Relation p57)

Edward Winslow was chosen to go across to speak to Massasoit using Squanto as an interpreter, to offer him some gifts of knives and a copper chain and greet him on behalf of King James. When this initial approach was well received, Winslow invited the Sachem to come to meet the leader of the English, their Governor, John Carver, and he agreed to stay as a hostage while this meeting took place. The meeting was a success and an agreement was reached between Massasoit and the English for mutual defence and co-existence as we have already described.

Although he made this agreement, Massasoit was clearly very afraid. It appears that Squanto had advised him that the English kept barrels in their store house, closely guarded and buried because they contained the plague. In fact it was the Pilgrims' store of gunpowder, but Massasoit was convinced that they had the means of totally destroying his people should they choose to. No wonder he seemed to be trembling with fear.

9. The First Thanksgiving

Just two weeks after the meeting with Massasoit, Captain Jones weighed anchor and took the Mayflower back on the long voyage to England. Soon after the Mayflower left, the streams around Plymouth became alive with fish, a Spring run of what the Pilgrims called 'herring'. Squanto who was still staying in the Hopkins' house, showed them that these fish were good to eat and had another even more important role to play. It was time to plant corn, not the wheat and barley familiar to the English, but the Indian Corn we also know as maize, the main food crop of the Native Americans.

They did try to grow some familiar crops, as Bradford reported:

'Some English seed they sowed, as wheat and peas, but it came not to good, either by the badness of the seed or lateness of the season or both, or some other defect.'
(William Bradford Ch XII)

Squanto showed them how to raise mounds of loose soil in the cleared areas and to plant corn in the mound, with a dead fish buried in the top to add fertility to the soil. Once the corn had sprouted and was growing strongly, he showed them how to plant climbing beans which used the corn stems for support. Finally, he showed them how to plant squash or pumpkins around the mounds to spread across the bare soil and smother weeds while producing a third crop.

All this was new to the Pilgrims. They had never seen the Native American way of using what are called 'the three sisters', corn, beans and squash as companion plants. The beans helped the corn to grow by fixing nitrogen in the soil; the corn supported the beans and the squash smothered the weeds at the edge of the mound.

The Three Sisters Garden
The reason we created a mini version of the "Three Sisters Garden" was so we can learn more about what the Native Americans ate and how they grew their food.

We got a seed-tray and we filled the pots with compost. We used a lollipop stick to make a hole in the compost to make room for the seed to go into and have room to grow. We planted beans, maize and pumpkin and kept them watered. We marked out the section in a corner of the playground where we needed to dig and dug it out. As we dug up the ground we found an old totem in the ground

that had smashed. The ground was very hard because it hadn't rained that much and the day was quite hot. If it was soft, the ground would be much easier to dig because we wouldn't have to be smashing the shovel into the ground. We found lots of roots in the ground which Darcy pulled out of the ground, which looked incredibly hard. There were lots of weeds in the ground which Olivia helpfully took out of the ground. We used a rake to dig up the earthy hard ground.

Finally we were ready to put fish, blood and bone meal on the ground around the plants to help them grow [Fish, blood and bone is like a food for the plants.] After that, we watered the plants with loads of water. It took five watering cans to get them up to scratch.

We looked after the plants for our last term of the year, and kept them watered. They grew really quickly in the summer heat!

After the summer in September 2019, we harvested some of our successful crops. These included the maize and the beans. Unfortunately, the other plants did not succeed, which showed us that it takes hard work, commitment and endurance to maintain a garden.

(by Studio5/6, St Helena's CofE School, Willoughby)

In the Pilgrims case, they had the New England climate and the help of Squanto to ensure a better crop, especially of pumpkins, but their 'pease' did not do well.

'We set the late spring some twenty acres of Indian Corn, and sowed some six acres of barley and pease, and according to the manner of the Indians, we manured our ground with herrings, or rather shads, which we have in great abundance and take with great ease at our doors. Our corn did prove well, and God be praised, we had a good increase of Indian corn, and our barley indifferent good, but our pease not worth the gathering, for we feared they were too late sown.....

(from Mourt's Relations p.82)

By October, as the trees were changing colour in the first Fall experienced by the Pilgrims, they gathered in the produce of their first planting and prepared to give thanks for their harvest. English Christians have celebrated Harvest time for centuries and the Pilgrims will have sensed a great thankfulness to God for their survival over almost their first year in the New World. It was time for a celebration.

'Our harvest being gotten in, our governor sent four men on fowling, so that we might after a special manner rejoice together after we had gathered the fruit of our labours. They four in one day killed as much fowl as, with a little help beside, served the company almost a week. At which time, amongst other recreation, we exercised our arms, many of the Indians coming amongst us, and among the rest their greatest King Massasoit, with some ninety men, whom for three days we entertained and feasted, and they went out and killed five deer, which they brought to the plantation and bestowed upon our governor, and upon the captain and others. And although it not always be so plentiful as it was at this time with us, yet by the goodness of God, we are so far from want that we often wish you partakers of our plenty.'

(Mourt's Relations p.82)

This celebration and thanksgiving has become the model for a great American National holiday, celebrated as Thanksgiving throughout the USA on the fourth Thursday in October, a time for families to get together and to share a meal. Today it is a non-denominational and secular holiday, a celebration of family, in the place of the original thanksgiving to God for survival. It was shared with the Wampanoag in gratitude for their help in surviving the first New England winter, the growing of food and the peace which they had agreed.

At St Helena's CofE School in Willoughby, we celebrated Thanksgiving with a turkey dinner, beans and pumpkin for the whole school, staff and children in November 2019, and used the party to launch our book, to parents, staff and friends of the school.

10. War breaks out

The English who were taken to Virginia, both at Jamestown and at Plymouth, worked as indentured servants for a period of years and then were given a grant of land to work for themselves. The Leiden Church had entered into an agreement with Weston and the Adventurers to work for so many days per week for the Company for the agreed number of years and then they, and the Strangers with no church link, were given their plot of land. The provision of a plot of land on which to build a home and to work for food was central to the establishment of Jamestown, Plymouth and to every other colonial settlement in America that followed. This land in the New World, offered by the King in England through the Company Charters was assumed '*not to be occupied by any Christian Prince*'. In other words no other European nation had got there first to take possession of the land.

The people who already lived there, the Native Americans who had occupied that land for hundreds if not thousands of years just did not count. They were not consulted and did not have the same sense of ownership of the land. It was only 'theirs' in the sense that they lived on it, loved it, left their dead on it or in it and made it part of their whole system of thought and belief. It was simply taken for the use of others, the European settlers coming into their areas in increasing numbers.

Ten years after the Pilgrims arrived at Plymouth, a much bigger group of English settlers arrived in the area which was to become the city of Boston. These were the Puritan emigrants organised by John Winthrop and financed through the Massachusetts Bay Company. Eleven ships, with 700 men women and children left Southampton in March 1630, bound for New England. John Winthrop's stirring speech to them just before they left, referred to Jesus' charge to his followers in Matthew 5 v14: '*You are the light of the world, a city set on a hill cannot be hid*'.

Winthrop told the Puritan settlers as they embarked on the Arbella, *'as a city set on a hill, the eyes of all people are upon us.'*

But, in the eyes of many Native American communities that image of a shining 'city on a hill' has become very tarnished over the centuries since 1620. Both in Virginia and in New England, the confederations of Native American Nations surrounding the initial European settlements watched the flow of English settlers coming into their home-lands. Eventually, in both areas, they came to the conclusion that they should drive out the English by force before it was too late. In Virginia, the Peace of Pocahontas held from her marriage to John Rolfe in 1614 to the massacre of settlers in 1622. In one day, Good Friday 1622, 347 settlers were killed on the scattered farms and settlements along the James River, about 25% of the total English settlers in Virginia at that time.

In New England, the time of peace lasted longer, from 1620 to the outbreak of the Pequot War of 1637. This was initially between the Massachusetts Bay settlements and the Pequot people of that area, but the Plymouth Colony sent men to fight with the Boston area settlers. In 1675, Massasoit second son, Metacom, also known as King Philip, led his Wampanoag people and their Narrangansett allies in attacks on colonial towns across the Cape Cod region. In the space of little more than a year, from June 1675 to August 1676, more than half of the English settlers' towns were attacked by Native Americans. Twelve were destroyed and many more damaged; the Plymouth Colony's economy was all but ruined. The English lost one-tenth of all men available for military service, about 600, and very many women and children.

But by the time that Metacom and his allies were defeated, the Native American had lost about 2,000 killed or died of wounds, 3,000 from sickness and starvation and 2,000 fled into other regions. A further 1,000 were captured alive and shipped out of New England as slaves to work on the sugar plantations of the

West Indies, where most soon died. Of the 20,000 Native Americans living in the region, somewhere between 60% and 80% were lost in what became known as King Philip's War, almost as many as had died in the Great Dying of the coastal Nations before 1620.

In terms of the proportion of deaths on both sides compared to total population, it was probably the deadliest war in the history of both England and North America. When King Philip was finally killed, as the Church record in Plymouth says: *'His head was brought into Plymouth in great triumph, he being slain two or three days before, so that in the day of our praises, our eyes saw the salvation of God.'* Just as the English in 17th Century London displayed the heads of those executed for rebellion or treason on poles on London Bridge, the head of Metacom, or King Philip, displayed on a pole above Plymouth fort became a grisly visitors' attraction long before interest focused on 'Plymouth Rock'.

The south end of London Bridge with the heads of traitors displayed on pikes much as the heads of 'King Philip' and his Native American fighters were displayed on pikes at the entrances to the towns of the Plymouth Colony.

After the intense fighting of King Philip's War, further conflict continued up to 1678, but the Native American communities in the region would never recover. Colonial New England did recover, but very slowly, taking a further hundred years for levels of prosperity to reach the pre-war level of 1675. Never again would Colonial English and Native American communities live as equals side by side. For some Narragansett leader's, even today, the conflict still goes on. As far as they are concerned, *'what the Puritans began here has never ended'*.

But trade did go on. Native American brought the furs and skins of the animals they trapped to trading centres to sell to the Colonial settlers. Beaver, bear, fox and deer-skins were traded for tools and guns, and for alcohol. The traditional form of currency used by the Native American, belts of *wampum* which were white or purple beads made from shells of whelks and clams, became the means of buying and selling, until dollar coins came into general use. In good years, Native American nations could also sell their surplus corn to settlements in both Virginia and New England.

But just as beavers had been wiped out in Europe by over-hunting, the supply of beaver pelts and other furs in New England ran out. When they had no more furs left to sell to the incomers, no food supplies or anything else that the settlers needed or wanted, they could only sell their land.

11. The Trail of Tears

For the English, it was always about land, land to the north and south of Plymouth Plantation where they could establish farms to grow their crops and graze their cattle. William Brewster had just such a farm at Duxbury to the north of Plymouth. On the James and the other Virginia rivers, it was land to plant tobacco so that great plantations and fine houses spread along the river-banks. At

Berkeley, Shirley and all the others, today's tourists walk where African slaves and rich English owners once lived, to serve the demand in England for Virginia tobacco.

Mostly, the English just took the land, displacing any Native Americans who happened to be using it for hunting or shifting agriculture. One of two exceptions was the Rev. Roger Williams, the Puritan Minister who was kicked out of the Massachusetts Colony for 'spreading new and dangerous ideas', and founded a new colony which became Rhode Island. He spent a lifetime trying to forge closer ties with the Wampanoag and especially the Narragansett tribes. The Narragansett deeded him the land for Providence city and, with the Wampanoag, helped the colony in its early months.

Williams's religious tract, *'Christenings make not Christians',* condemned mass Indian conversions. He preached the gospel and lived the Christian life as an example to them, but he also believed they had the right to worship as they wished. Williams admired the Indians but never romanticized them. He believed that Native Americans who lost their land should receive compensation, but he also knew that they could be both noble and "insolent." And he was English first of all: he headed a militia during King Philip's War, and then helped to sell Indian captives as slaves to raise money for English families who lost homes in the war.

The second leader of an English Colony who believed that the Native Americans should be compensated for the loss of their lands was the Quaker, William Penn. In 1681, Charles II signed a charter granting territory west of the Delaware River and north of Maryland, approximately the present size of Pennsylvania, to William Penn. The King proposed the name "Pennsylvania" to honour Penn's late father, who was an Admiral in Charles' Navy. Penn would be the proprietor, owning all the land, accountable directly to the King. At the beginning of each year, Penn had to give the King two beaver skins and a fifth of any gold and silver mined within the territory.

Penn's Colony offered an American sanctuary which protected freedom of conscience for both settlers and Native Americans. Almost everywhere else, colonists stole land from the Native Americans, but Penn travelled unarmed among the Delaware and negotiated peaceful purchases of land. He insisted that women deserved equal rights with men, noting that in Native American communities, women often mediated in disputes. Penn agreed a sum to be paid to the Delaware Nation in compensation for their land and, before he left Pennsylvania to return to England, had signed a treaty with the Delaware.

All along the north-east coast of the North American continent, the English established colonies, thirteen of them. By 1775, the total population of these settlements had grown to about 2.4 million, mainly English but also Dutch and German, and an increasing number of slaves of African origin, all living in English-led colonies. The original Native American population had been forced out, pushed ever west-wards over the Appalachian mountains, or absorbed in small and dwindling pockets of land accepted as 'Indian Reservations' within the thirteen colonies.

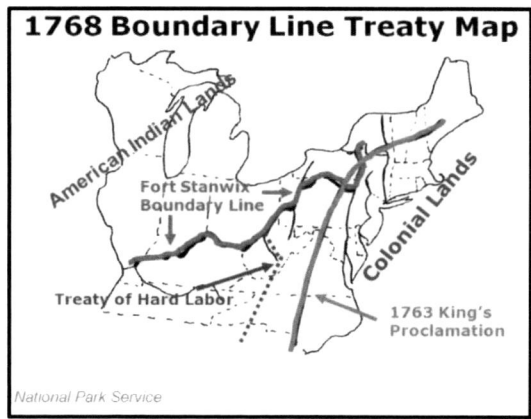

1768 Boundary Line Treaty Map

American Indian Lands

Fort Stanwix Boundary Line

Treaty of Hard Labor

Colonial Lands

1763 King's Proclamation

National Park Service

After the British defeated the French in North America, King George III issued a proclamation in 1763 that created a boundary line between the British colonies on the Atlantic coast and American Indian lands (called the 'Indian Reserve') west of the Appalachian Mountains.

The proclamation line was not intended to be a permanent boundary between the colonists and Native American lands, but rather a temporary boundary which could be extended further west in an orderly, lawful manner, but it did not last long.

The American War of Independence broke out in 1775 and by 1783, George Washington, with some help from the French, had defeated the British, before becoming the first President of the United States of America.

Twenty five years earlier, the British had signed a treaty with the Native American Iroquois League that held the land beyond the King's proclamation to honour their occupation of this land up to the red line of the Fort Stanwix boundary. They had also agreed with the Cherokee that they should continue to occupy the land beyond the blue dotted line, in what became known as the Treaty of Hard Labour.

But when the British were defeated along with their Native American allies, the victorious Americans renegotiated the Fort Stanwix boundary, so that the Iroquois lost the land south of the Ohio River, establishing a pattern which saw more and more 'Indian Land' released for white settlement.

Eventually, all the land east of the Mississippi River which had been occupied by Native American nations was opened to occupation by white settlers and the original occupants became the 'Indian problem'. The solution to this problem, agreed by the US Congress, was that they should simply move, following 1830, in a series of forced migrations, one nation after another from their homelands east of the river to new homes beyond the rive to the west.

The Indian Removal Act was signed into law on May 28, 1830, by United States President, Andrew Jackson. The law authorized the President to negotiate with southern Native American tribes for their removal to federal territory west of the Mississippi River in exchange for white settlement of their ancestral lands. 'Negotiate' was a sham as the President and Congress had already agreed that they had to go. A few went peacefully, but the majority who resisted were given no choice, forced to move and given little help.

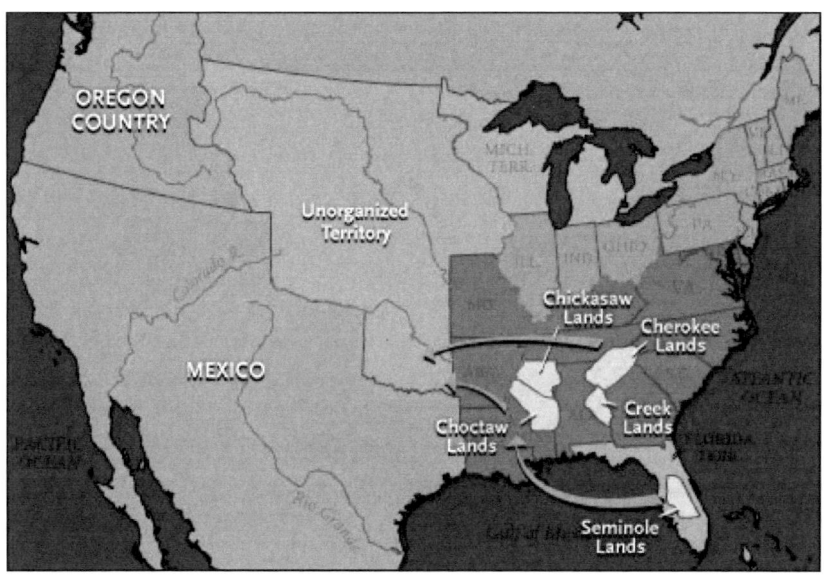

The removal of Native American nations to beyond the Mississippi

The Choctaw were moved in 1831. The Seminole began to be removed from Florida in 1632 but it would take twenty years to complete their removal. The removal of the Creek started in 1834. and the Chickasaw voluntarily moved in 1837. All these nations suffered during the removal. Some were taken by boat along the river system, but most had to walk with little food and no transport.

Of all the nations, the 16,000 Cherokee suffered most. They had occupied land in what became the State of Georgia for thousands of years, but cotton growing had encroached on their land, with the support of the State of Georgia. The Cherokee took

73

the State to the Supreme Court and won; the U.S. Supreme Court affirming that native nations were sovereign nations "in which the laws of Georgia [and other states] can have no force." Even so, the encroachment continued. As President Andrew Jackson noted in 1832, if no one intended to enforce the Supreme Court's rulings (which he certainly did not), then the decisions would fall. Southern states were determined to take ownership of Native American lands and would go to great lengths to secure this territory. When gold was discovered in Georgia, the clamour to solve the 'Indian Problem' by removal could not be ignored.

But by 1838, only about 2,000 Cherokees had left their Georgia homeland for Indian territory. President Martin Van Buren sent General Winfield Scott and 7,000 soldiers to speed up the removal process. Scott and his troops forced the Cherokee into stockades at bayonet point while whites looted their homes and belongings.

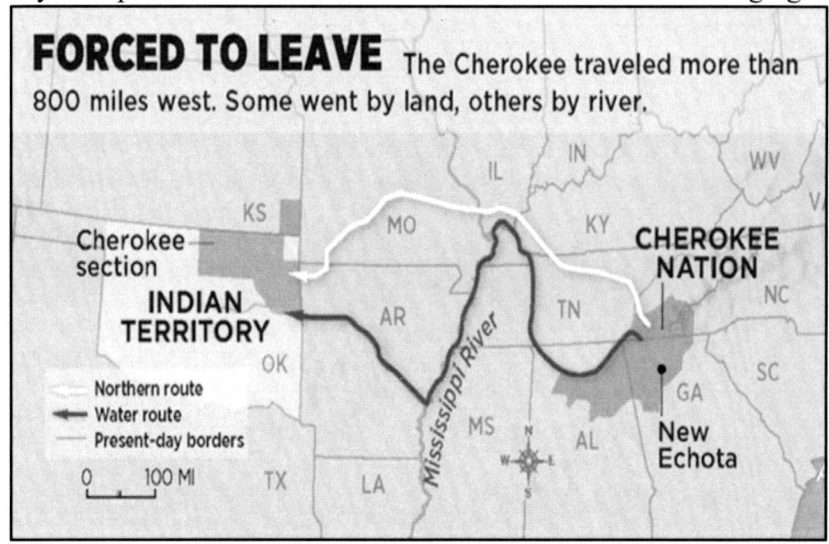

FORCED TO LEAVE The Cherokee traveled more than 800 miles west. Some went by land, others by river.

Then, they marched the Cherokee people more than 800 miles to the west, beyond the Mississippi River to an area designated as 'Indian territory'. Whooping cough, typhus, dysentery, cholera and starvation were epidemic along the way, and historians estimate that more than 5,000 Cherokee died as a result of the journey. The Cherokee were farming people and they could not take enough food with them, or gather enough along the way, to avoid starvation.

The Cherokee Trail of Tears

By 1840, tens of thousands of Native Americans had been driven off of their land in the south-eastern states and forced to move across the Mississippi to 'Indian territory'. The federal government promised that their new land would remain theirs and they would be unmolested forever, but as the line of white settlement pushed westward, 'Indian country' shrank and went on shrinking. In 1907, Oklahoma became a state and Indian territory was gone for good.

On the west, Pacific, coast, the Native American nations faced a flood of prospectors to the gold-fields of California. Their number in that State dropped from 150,000 in 1845 to 35,000, living on the poor lands set aside as reservations. In Oregon and Washington State, the US Army fought a series of bloody wars in the 1850s to force Native Americans onto reservations. In Arizona and New Mexico, the Army struggled to assert its authority throughout the 1850s and on the southern plains, mounted warriors of the Sioux, Cheyenne, Arapahos, Comanches and Kiowas harassed isolated white settlements.

In the 1860s, during the American Civil War, seven Native American regiments served with Confederate troops but ended up on the losing side. After the war, former Union soldiers, like Kit Carson, fought a ruthlessly effective campaign against the Navahos in New Mexico and Arizona. Regiments of black soldiers in the Union Army moved west at the end of the war, and became known as 'buffalo soldiers' due to their curly hair. Their role was to protect Native American of the 'civilised tribes' in their reservations, but also to make sure that they stayed there.

But the relentless expansion west of mining, railways, demand for land and the loss of the herds of buffalo from the Plains, reignited old tensions. The US Cavalry destroyed Native American settlements, slaughtered their ponies and cut off their food supplies, but the Native Americans fought back. A loose alliance of Sioux, Northern Cheyenne, and Arapahos under Crazy Horse and Sitting Bull met the US Cavalry at the Little Bighorn, resulting in the famous battle and the annihilation of five troops of Custer's cavalry.

Such major successes were rare though and eventually, the tribes sued for peace and accepted reservation life. One final outbreak of war by the Sioux and the Northern Cheyenne led to the massacre at Wounded Knee, where over two hundred Native American men, women and children of the Latoka Sioux people died and twenty four soldiers died. Amongst the dead were eight Sioux babies.

The major conflicts had ended. In the end, however, military force alone had not destroyed Native American resistance. Only with the combination of railroad expansion, the destruction of the buffalo, increased numbers of settlers, and the determination of successive US governments to crush any challenge to their authority, had white armies overwhelmed the tribes.

12. Chief Seattle's lament

White Americans had spread across the Continent pushing the Native Americans into smaller and smaller 'Reservations', and further and further west and north, until most of America was taken away from the Native Americans for use by white men. Towards the end of that process, in the 1850s and in the far north-west of the United States, a Native American Chief by the name of Seattle is said to have given a speech on the occasion of the last selling of the land of his Nation.

'How can you buy or sell the sky, the warmth of the land? The idea is strange to us....The rivers are our brothers....The air is precious...for all things share the same breath and this we know. The earth does not belong to man. Man belongs to the earth. This we know. All things are connected like the blood which unites one family.'

These words have become the best known part of the 'Chief Seattle's speech'. But we now know that they were not in fact part of the original version. These words were written by a white screen-writer for a film in the 1970s. The author was not even of Native American heritage and although the spirit of what he wrote is in tune with the original speech, they do not reflect Seattle's key concern. He was asking that his people should have free access to the places where their forefathers had died.

It was in 1854 that the Chief of the Lushootseed people and the Governor of the most North-Western of the States of the USA, Washington State, entered into a treaty to sell Native American land to white settlers. It was one of the last times that a Native American people sold their land to white Americans. The Native American Chief, who has become known as Chief Seattle, spoke with great dignity in his own language. Someone translated this into another Native American language and a third translated it into English. This is part of what Chief Seattle is believed to have actually said, and in our book about Mayflower 400, we give the last word to Chief Seattle and his American Indian people:

'Yonder sky that has wept tears of compassion upon my people for centuries untold, and which to us appears changeless and eternal, may change. Today is fair. Tomorrow it may be overcast with clouds. My words are like the stars that never change. Whatever Seattle says, the great chief at Washington can rely upon with as much certainty as he can upon the return of the sun or the seasons.

The white chief says that Big Chief at Washington sends us greetings of friendship and goodwill. This is kind of him for we know he has little need of our friendship in return. His people are many. They are like the grass that covers vast prairies. My people are few. They resemble the scattering trees of a storm-swept plain. The great, and I presume good, White Chief sends us word that he wishes to buy our land but is willing to allow us enough to live comfortably. This indeed appears just, even generous, for the Red Man no longer has rights that he need respect, and the offer may be wise, also, as we are no longer in need of an extensive country.

There was a time when our people covered the land as the waves of a wind-ruffled sea cover its shell-paved floor, but that time long since passed away with the greatness of tribes that are now but a mournful memory. .....

Your God is not our God! Your God loves your people and hates mine! He folds his strong protecting arms lovingly about the paleface and leads him by the hand as a father leads an infant son. But, He has forsaken His Red children, if they really are His. Our God, the Great Spirit, seems also to have forsaken us. Your God makes your people wax stronger every day. Soon they will fill all the land. Our people are ebbing away like a rapidly receding tide that will never return...............

To us the ashes of our ancestors are sacred and their resting place is hallowed ground. You wander far from the graves of your ancestors and seemingly without regret. ... Our dead never forget this beautiful world that gave them being. They still love its verdant valleys, its murmuring rivers, its magnificent mountains, ...and often return from the happy hunting ground to visit, guide, console, and comfort them.......

We will ponder your proposition and when we decide we will let you know. But should we accept it, I here and now make this condition that we will not be denied the privilege without molestation of visiting at any time the tombs of our ancestors, friends, and children. Every part of this soil is sacred in the estimation of my people. Every hillside, every valley, every plain and grove, has been hallowed by some sad or happy event in days long vanished. Even the rocks, which seem to be dumb and dead as they swelter in the sun along the silent shore, thrill with memories of stirring events connected with the lives of my people,

And when the last Red Man shall have perished, and the memory of my tribe shall have become a myth among the White Men, these shores will swarm with the invisible dead of my tribe, and when your children's children think themselves alone in the field, the store, the shop, upon the highway, or in the silence of the pathless woods, they will not be alone. ... At night when the streets of your cities and villages are silent and you think them deserted, they will throng with the returning hosts that once filled them and still love this beautiful land. The White Man will never be alone.

Let him be just and deal kindly with my people, for the dead are not powerless. Dead, did I say? There is no death, only a change of worlds.'

(Chief Seattle of the Lushootseed people, 1854)

Sources and Thanks

We used a wide range of sources, printed and on-line to research this book and especially the following ARIES books: 'Admiral of New England – Captain John Smith and the American Dream', 'Mrs John Rolfe of Heacham – better known as Pocahontas'. 'Robert Troublechurch Browne of Tolethorpe and the Separatist Movement', 'William Brewster of the Pilgrim Fathers', all published by Barny Books and involving work with Primary Schools.

The project was supported by the Staff and Governors of St Helena's CofE School, Willoughby and especially by Mrs Sue Belton, Headteacher, and Mr Joshua Goddard, Studio 5/6 Teacher.

The pupils of Studio 5/6 worked on the project, and work from an earlier book with Heacham Junior School, Norfolk is also included.

We would like to thank them all.

Mayflower 400 -
but what about the
Native Americans?

by

John Haden and the Pupils of
St Helena's CofE Primary School,
Willoughby, Lincolnshire

ISBN No: 978-1-912082-59-9
Publishers: Barny Books
              76 Cotgrave Lane, Tollerton, NG32 2HL
              Tel: +44(0)115 937 5147
              www.barnybooks.co.uk/

Copies of this book and the others in the Books with Schools and
ARIES series may be obtained from the Publisher or from:

              Books with Schools Project
              13 St Albans Close, Oakham
              Rutland LE15 6EW
              Tel: 01572 720428

Contents

Corrections: please note that 'Clatford All Saints' should read 'Upper Clatford' on line 26 page 48 and '13th April 1581' should read '30th April 1581 on line 29 page 48, with apologies for errors.

1. 'No trespassing!'

The English street artist known as Banksy went to San Francisco in the USA in 2010 and left a piece of art on a wall.

The small 'No Trespassing' sign was already on the wall. It reminds us of the way our laws and the laws of the United States of America give rights to land owners, including the right to exclude others from their property. Banksy added the image of the Native American, sitting on the pavement looking sad, dressed in a cloth and a few feathers. He is a representative of all the people who once occupied the continents of America, North and South, those who were there before any Europeans arrived on their shores.